Discovering

TREES

Jill Bailey

Illustrated by Wendy Meadway

The Bookwright Press
New York · 1989

5592

Discovering Nature

Discovering Ants
Discovering Bees and Wasps
Discovering Beetles
Discovering Birds of Prey
Discovering Bugs
Discovering Butterflies and Moths
Discovering Crabs and Lobsters
Discovering Crickets and Grasshoppers
Discovering Damselflies and
    Dragonflies
Discovering Ducks, Geese and Swans

Discovering Flies
Discovering Flowering Plants
Discovering Freshwater Fish
Discovering Frogs and Toads
Discovering Rabbits and Hares
Discovering Rats and Mice
Discovering Sea Birds
Discovering Slugs and Snails
Discovering Snakes and Lizards
Discovering Spiders
Discovering Squirrels
Discovering Trees
Discovering Worms

First published in the
United States in 1989 by
The Bookwright Press
387 Park Avenue South
New York, NY 10016

First published in 1988 by
Wayland (Publishers) Limited
61 Western Road, Hove
East Sussex BN3 1JD, England

© Copyright 1988 Wayland (Publishers) Limited

Typeset by DP Press Ltd., Sevenoaks, Kent
Printed in Italy by Sagdos S.p.A., Milan

Cover *A tree stands in the middle of a field of brilliant yellow mustard.*

Frontispiece *The Lawson cypress from North America grows to 40 meters (131 feet) in height. It has a narrow, conical crown and drooping leaves.*

Library of Congress Cataloging-in-Publication Data

Bailey, Jill
  [Discovering trees]
  Trees / by Jill Bailey
     p. cm.—(Discovering nature)
  First published in 1988 in England under title: Discovering trees.
  Bibliography: p.
  Includes index.
  Summary: Provides a botanical account of trees, examining their life processes, different types, and ecology.
  ISBN 0–531–18228–2
  1. Trees—Juvenile literature. [1. Trees.]   I. Title.
II Series.
  QB475.8.B35 1989
  582.16—dc19

88–19376
CIP
AC

Contents

1 Introducing Trees
What Do Trees Look Like? *8*
Broad-leaved Trees *10*
Conifer Trees *12*

2 How Trees Work
Leaves *14*
Stems and Roots *16*

3 Making New Trees
How Do Trees Grow? *18*
Flowers *20*
Pollination *22*
Fruits and Seeds *24*

4 Where Do You Find Trees?
Trees Near Our Homes *26*
Forests *28*

5 Trees and Humans
Trees That Feed Us *30*
Wood That Works For Us *32*

6 Friends and Enemies
Life in a Big Tree *34*
Enemies of Trees *36*
The Death of a Tree *38*

7 Learning More About Trees *40*

Glossary *44*
Finding Out More *45*
Index *46*

1
Introducing Trees

An Australian ghost gum tree with its slender trunk and leafy crown.

What Do Trees Look Like?

A tree is a very large plant supported by a woody stem. It has branching roots that grow down into the soil to anchor it, and a branching stem, called the **trunk**, with green leaves or needles. At certain times of the year, a tree produces **cones** or flowers, which later develop into seeds, fruits or nuts.

Trees can live for many years. As a tree grows bigger and bigger, the trunk gets fatter as more wood is produced. This helps to support its increasing weight. A tough outer layer of corky **bark** helps to protect the tree from attack by enemies such as insects and **fungi**.

Some trees live for a very long time. There are bristlecone pines in the United States that are over 4,500 years old, and some California redwoods may be 6,000 years old. The largest living thing in the world is a giant

redwood tree called Major Sherman. This tree is 83.8 meters (275 feet) tall and measures 34.9 meters (115 feet) around its trunk. It weighs over 2,700 tons, which is 1,300 billion times more than the weight of the seed it has grown from.

The Australian gum trees are among the tallest and fastest-growing trees in the world. They can grow an astonishing 10.6 meters (35 feet) in a year, and eventually may reach heights of over 122 meters (400 feet).

Trees have been around for a very long time. The oldest known fossil trees date from 180,000,000 years ago. These are the ancestors of the ginkgos of China, which are very graceful trees with drooping branches and wavy leaves.

Bristlecone pines live for a very long time. Some of them are over 4,500 years old.

Broad-leaved Trees

There are two main kinds of trees, the broad-leaved trees and the **conifers**. The broad-leaved trees produce flowers, but the conifers produce cones instead.

Leaves come in many different shades of green. Young leaves are usually bright green and become

Elm trees are deciduous, so in winter you can see their bare outline.

darker and duller as they grow older. Some trees, such as holly and laurel, have shiny leaves covered with wax. This keeps the leaves from losing too much water. Trees that grow in hot, dry climates often have shiny leaves.

Many broad-leaved trees shed their leaves in winter, or during very dry weather. We call these **deciduous** trees. By shedding their leaves, the trees save precious water. They need water in winter, when the roots are so cold that they cannot work fast enough to take up much water, or when the water in the soil is frozen. At this time, next year's leaves are already forming inside the buds, protected by a tough, waterproof cover of **bud scales**.

The leaves of deciduous trees turn beautiful shades of red, gold and brown in autumn. This happens when the trees are reaching the end of their food-making cycle, and their green

chlorophyll gradually disappears.

Take a close look at the bare trees in winter, and see if you can spot their different shapes. Is there a long main trunk, or does the trunk branch quite low down? Do the branches turn up or down at the tips?

Above *Beech leaves turn gradually from green to beautiful shades of red, gold and brown in autumn.*

Left *The sun shines through the fresh green leaves of a beech and oak wood in spring.*

Conifer Trees

Conifers are very tough trees. They are found in cold climates and at greater mountain heights than most other kinds of trees. They are often pyramid-shaped, with flexible branches that curve downward. This helps the snow slide off in winter.

Conifers produce cones instead of flowers. Cones are rather like clusters of tiny woody flowers. Each cone is made up of tough scales, which carry the male or female parts of the flower. The male cones produce pollen, while the female cones contain the plant's eggs, which will later develop into seeds. In some conifers the cones hang down when they are ripe, while in others they point upward.

Different conifers produce different shapes and sizes of cones. Some junipers have tiny cones, while the sugar pine of the United States has

Some of the giant redwood trees are 6,000 years old.

cones up to 50 cm (20 in) long. Fir cones are long and sausage-shaped; cypress cones are small and round.

Yew trees do not produce proper cones. Instead, their seeds are surrounded by a bright red fleshy cup, and look rather like berries.

The leaves of most conifers are either long, thin **needles**, like the leaves of the pine, spruce and fir, or small, triangular scalelike leaves, like those of the cypress. These scaly leaves overlap closely to cover the whole twig. The needles grow either in tufts, or along the twigs in fringes.

Most conifers keep their leaves all year round and so they are called **evergreen** trees. A few, such as the larches, shed their leaves in autumn.

The pine tree has tufts of needle-shaped leaves and cones instead of flowers.

Yew trees produce red fleshy cups to surround their seeds.

2
How Trees Work

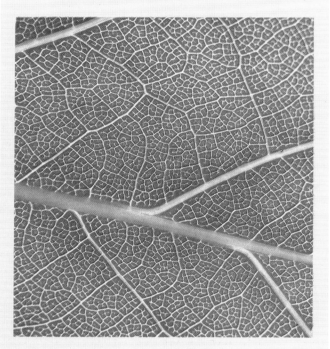

The network of fine veins in a leaf carries water to the leaves and the food made by photosynthesis to the rest of the tree.

Leaves

All the material that goes to make up a tree is produced by the tree itself. To do this, it needs the leaves. The green substance in the leaves, chlorophyll, absorbs energy from sunlight. The leaves use this energy to combine simple chemicals (**carbon dioxide** and water) to make plant material. This special process is called **photosynthesis**.

Carbon dioxide is a gas found in the air. It enters the leaves through tiny holes in the surface, called **stomata**. Water and minerals are brought to the leaves from the roots through a system of tiny tubes, which branch out all over the leaf to form the veins. The food that is made in the leaves by photosynthesis is carried to the rest of the plant in these veins.

Photosynthesis produces **oxygen**, a gas that animals and humans need

for breathing. Without green plants, there would not be enough oxygen in the air for us to survive. The oxygen passes out of the leaf through the stomata and enters the air. Water can also escape from the plant in this way, but if the plant is short of water, the stomata close up to save it .

The leaves need to trap sunlight,

Leaves arrange themselves so that they overlap as little as possible, to absorb a lot of sunlight.

and so it is important that they are not shaded. Leaves twist their stalks so that they face directly into the sun, and are often arranged so that they do not overlap each other.

Stems and Roots

The roots of the tree grow down into the soil to anchor it. Without roots, the tree would easily be blown over by the wind. As the trunk and branches grow, the roots grow, too.

The roots are also important because they take in water and minerals from the soil. The water helps to keep the leaves stiff. The tiny **cells** that make up the leaves are

The dark rings of autumn growth and the light rings of spring wood are clear in the trunk of this old pine tree.

The knobby roots of an old beech tree.

like little bags full of water. The water keeps the bags stiff. If the tree loses too much water, the cells become floppy, and then the leaves cannot spread out to catch the sunlight.

A system of tiny tubes carries water and minerals from the roots to the leaves for photosynthesis, and food from the leaves to the roots to help them grow.

The wood of the trunk supports the water-carrying tubes so that they do not collapse under the tree's weight. As the tree grows taller, the trunk gets fatter, because more layers of wood are added to it.

In autumn, when the tree does not grow as fast, the new tubes produced are smaller than the tubes produced in spring. They are far too small for you to see, but when you look at a fallen tree trunk, you can see light and dark rings of wood. The dark rings are the autumn wood, and the light rings the spring wood. By counting the rings, you can tell the age of the tree.

INSIDE A TREE TRUNK

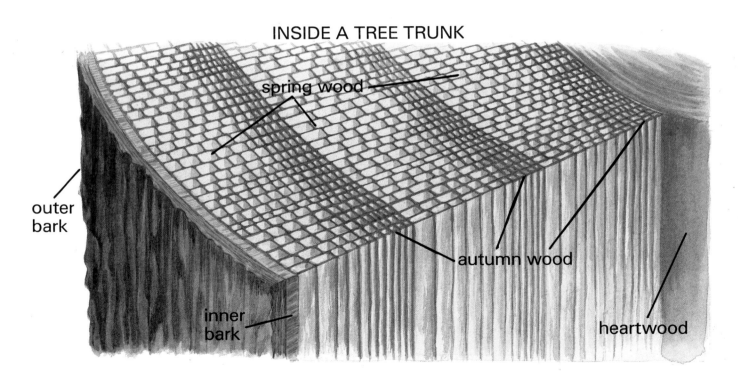

outer bark

inner bark

spring wood

autumn wood

heartwood

3
Making New Trees

Among the mosses on a woodland floor, an oak seedling sprouts from an acorn, breaking open the outer shell.

How Do Trees Grow?

A tree starts its life as a seed. The seed contains a tiny plant, surrounded by a store of food and a tough coat that protects it from bad weather. The seed soaks up water from the soil and swells until it bursts through its coat. Now it starts to grow, using its store of food. It puts out a tiny root, which grows down into the soil, and a tiny shoot, which bends up toward the light of the sun.

Baby tree **seedlings** look quite different from their parents. The first leaves to open are often a very different shape from the later ones. We call them **seed leaves**.

Unlike humans, trees grow all through their lives. A tree grows in two ways. It grows taller by adding on to the tips of the twigs every year, and it grows fatter by adding layers of wood around the twigs and trunk.

The roots also grow longer and fatter.

In climates where there are different seasons, trees do most of their growing in the spring and summer. The buds burst open, and new leaves unfold. These leaves make their own food, with enough to spare to make new leaves and flowers.

Trees are different shapes because they have different patterns of growth. Some trees have a wide, spreading **crown** of branches, where

These larches on the banks of a Scottish loch have grown into strange flattened shapes because of the strong winds.

all the branches grow at much the same rate. Others have narrow, pointed crowns, where the tip of the main trunk grows faster than the side branches. Trees that grow in windy places often become twisted as they grow because the branches facing away from the wind grow fastest.

Flowers

When a tree reaches a certain age, it starts to produce flowers or cones. These contain the male and female parts that produce **seeds**.

Flowers come in many shapes, but they all have the same parts. In the center is the female part, the **pistil**. The pistil is the seed-bearing organ. It is made up of one or more **carpels** in which the seeds grow. Each carpel has three parts: the **ovary** at the bottom,

The center of a flower contains the carpel, surrounded by the stamens.

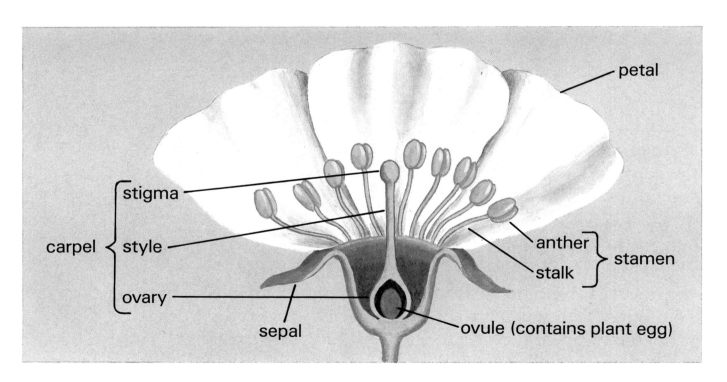

where the seeds are formed; the **style**, a slender spike that extends from the ovary; and the **stigma**, a sticky pad at the tip of each style, where the pollen settles.

The male parts, or **stamens**, are arranged in a ring around the carpels. Each stamen bears a little bag of pollen, called an **anther**, on a long stalk. When the stamen is ripe, the anther bursts open, and a cloud of yellow powdery pollen escapes.

This tropical poui tree produces masses of small pink flowers.

Outside the stamens are the petals, and surrounding the petals are the leaflike **sepals**, which protect the flower while it is in bud.

For a seed to be produced, pollen from an anther must land on the sticky stigma of a flower. The pollen grows down through the style to the ovary to **fertilize** the egg cells there.

Pollination

The transferring of pollen from one flower or cone to another is called **pollination**. Cones and some flowers rely on the wind to do this. They produce masses of tiny pollen grains that float on the breeze until they land on the stigma of another flower.

Below *A honey bee feeds on the nectar in some apple blossom.*

Above *The wind will carry the pollen from these birch catkins to the female flower.*

Wind-pollinated flowers are often dull colored, with tiny green or brown petals. Some trees produce long, dangling catkins, which wave around in the breeze.

Other flowers use insects or other animals to carry their pollen for them. These flowers often have brightly colored petals to attract attention, and at the base of the petals there are tiny cups full of a sweet-smelling sugary liquid, called **nectar**.

Insects such as bees, butterflies and moths are attracted to the flowers by their bright color and sweet smell, and feed on the nectar and pollen. Some flowers have brightly colored centers to help the insects find the nectar and pollen.

As the insects feed, pollen is trapped on the hairs on their bodies. As they enter the next flower, the pollen rubs off against its stigma.

Some trees, like the tulip tree and the magnolia, produce flowers that stand alone on the twigs. Others, such as the cherry tree, produce masses of tiny flowers in large clusters.

A pollen grain grows down inside the stigma to the ovary.

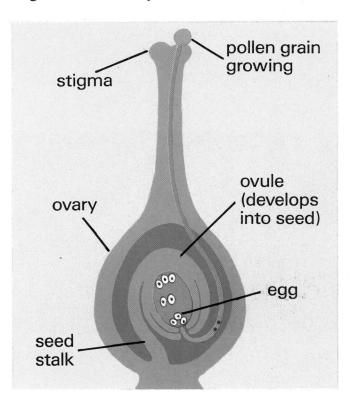

Fruits and Seeds

After a flower has been fertilized, seeds start to form inside its ovaries. At the same time, other parts of the flower begin to change to form the **fruit**, which will surround the seeds.

In apples, pears, plums and cherries, the fleshy stem immediately below the flower swells until it surrounds the seeds. The outer skin of the fruit turns red. This attracts birds and other animals, which eat the fruit. The seeds are not digested, and pass out of the animal with its droppings. In this way, the seeds are spread to new places. Yew trees enclose their seeds in a red fleshy cup, and some trees, such as hawthorn and holly, produce clusters of shiny red berries.

Many trees produce nuts, which are eaten by squirrels and other animals.

The fruits of the red maple have rosy-colored wings to help them travel long distances on the wind.

Many trees, such as oak, hazel and hickory, produce nuts. The ovary wall becomes very hard. Animals, such as mice, squirrels, jays and woodpeckers, carry off the nuts to feed on the food stored inside the shells.

The fruit of the maple and sycamore has a flat, papery wing attached to it when it falls off the tree. This is the ovary wall. This wing makes the fruit spin around and around like the blades of a helicopter, and helps it to travel a long way on the wind. The seeds of pine trees have no outer case but do have papery wings. Kapok and willow also use the wind to carry away their seeds. Each seed has its own fluffy white parachute to carry it along.

The coconut uses the sea to carry its seeds to faraway shores. The coconut husk is very light. Air trapped between the hairs of the husk helps the coconut to float.

A coconut seed, having been carried miles by the sea, sprouts on a tropical beach.

25

4
Where Do You Find Trees?

On open farmland an old oak tree makes shade for animals in summer.

Trees Near Our Homes

Trees are found almost everywhere that people live. We plant trees in our yards because we find them beautiful to look at, or because we want birds and other animals near our houses.

Trees or hedges planted around the edge of a backyard prevent other people from watching everything we do. In cities, trees are planted to hide ugly buildings, and to make streets look more attractive.

In hot countries, people plant trees to give them shade. Even in cooler parts of the world, trees are often planted in fields to give animals a shady resting place in summer.

In England the countryside is often divided up by **hedgerows** made of trees that have been cut and trained in a special way. The hedgerows keep animals from straying from one field to another, and also help to prevent

the soil from blowing away.

Closely planted rows of trees provide shelter from the wind for animals and farmhouses. Certain kinds of trees may be planted on sand dunes to stop the sand from blowing over nearby houses and roads, or to prevent it from blowing away

Cherry trees in blossom make suburban roads look beautiful in springtime.

altogether, letting in the sea.

People admire trees so much that they often plant a tree to celebrate an important public event, such as the opening of a big new building or park.

Forests

Vast areas of the earth's surface are covered with forests. There are many kinds of forests all over the world. In the far north, and on high mountains, the forests contain mainly evergreen conifers. These are dark forests, where very little light reaches the forest floor at any time of the year, which means that few flowers can grow beneath the trees.

Farther south, the forests contain mainly broad-leaved trees. These allow more light to reach the forest floor. In early spring, before the new leaves open, the forest floor is covered with wild flowers. In autumn, the

The pine forests of Tenerife spread high up the mountainsides.

Bald cypress trees grow in the swamps of the Atchafalaya Basin in Louisiana.

forests turn gold, yellow and brown, and the trees gradually drop their leaves, so in winter most of the trees are bare.

In the warm, moist tropics, rain forests grow. Here there is no clear change of season, so trees may produce new leaves and flowers at any time of the year. These are forests where the plants are dense, with several layers of growth, including trees and shrubs, vines trailing from the trees, and a thick tangle of plants covering the forest floor.

Trees also grow in swampy areas. Around the coasts of the warmer parts of the world, mangrove swamps have developed. The bases of the mangrove trees are under water for much of the time, so some of their roots stick up into the air to breathe, or trail down from the trunk into the water. In the southern United States, the swamp cypress has similar breathing roots.

The dense vegetation of the tropical rain forest of Panama.

5

Trees and Humans

The large pink pods of the cocoa tree grow out of the trunk.

Trees That Feed Us

Many of the things we eat come from trees. Fruits like apples, pears, plums, cherries, olives, oranges and lemons all grow on trees. Dates are the fruits of date palms, and coconuts grow on coconut palms.

Nuts, such as walnuts, Brazil nuts, cashews, pistachios, pecans, hickories, and many others, are also the fruits of trees. A tree's seeds are protected by the nuts' hard outer shells.

Some of our drinks come from trees. Coffee comes from the fruits of the coffee tree, cocoa from the pods of the cocoa tree, and tea is made from the dried leaves of the tea tree, which is grown mainly in regions of India, Sri Lanka and China.

Trees also provide us with oils. Palm oil comes from the fruit of the oil palm, and is the main ingredient in soap. Olive oil is used in cooking and

in salad dressing, and was once burned in lamps.

Maple syrup comes from the **sap** of the sugar maple. In spring, when the sap is rising, a cut is made in the bark, and as the sap runs out it is collected in a bucket that is tied onto the trunk.

Spices like cloves and nutmeg come from the fruits of trees, and cinnamon comes from the bark of the cinnamon tree. The dried leaves of the bay laurel are used in cooking, usually to flavor stews and soups.

Food trees, like apple and plum trees, are grown in orchards. Date palms, orange and olive trees are grown in large groves in the tropics. Here, they can be carefully looked after so that they will produce larger, healthier crops than when they grow in the wild.

Dates hang in great bundles from this date palm on the Blue Nile in Sudan.

Wood That Works For Us

Wood is an extremely useful material. We use it to make houses, sheds, fences, gates, packing cases, furniture and boats. This kind of wood comes mainly from broad-leaved trees.

Certain conifers, such as pines, grow with tall, straight trunks and very few branches, particularly if they are grown close together. These trunks are ideal for making telephone poles.

Even the paper in this book is made from wood, mainly from conifer wood, which has been mashed up and rolled out flat. Wood is also used to make matches, toothpicks and chopsticks, as well as hundreds of other objects for everyday use.

In the developing world, wood is burned for cooking and for keeping warm. For millions of poor people, who have no electricity or gas

The sap of the rubber tree is collected in buckets as it runs out of the trunk.

supply, burning wood is their only source of heat. This is causing great problems as the world's population is increasing and more and more of the great forests are being cut down and used for firewood.

Tree trunks produce other useful materials, too. Cork is the bark of the cork oak. Rubber comes from the sap of the rubber tree. Other kinds of trees

Wood is collected from the forests in Brazil to be used as firewood.

have channels full of **resin**, a sticky gum, in their trunks. The resins are taken from the trees and are used in making paints, varnishes, lacquers and gums. Many important medicines have been produced from chemicals found in tropical trees.

6
Friends and Enemies

Trees are often the home of plants, such as ivy, that grow over the trunk.

Life in a Big Tree

Trees provide food for many animals. Deer browse on the lower branches, caterpillars feed on buds and leaves, and birds feed on the caterpillars. In the tropics, leaf-cutter ants climb the trees to cut off pieces of leaf, which they take back to their underground nests. Bees and butterflies visit the tree's flowers to feed on nectar, and troops of monkeys swing from tree to tree in search of ripe fruit.

All sorts of animals make their homes in the trunks of trees hollowed out by decay. Woodpeckers, starlings, owls, and more exotic birds such as toucans and parrots like to nest in hollow trees, out of sight of their enemies. Bats roost in hollow trees, and wild bees and wasps build their nests in them.

Bigger animals, such as raccoons, also live in tree hollows, and mice, rats and foxes make their homes under the twisting roots. The animals line their nests with dry leaves and moss, which they take from the tree.

Smaller creatures like beetles, spiders and centipedes live in crevices in the bark, and woodpeckers and nuthatches come to feed on them. Birds and squirrels build their nests among the branches.

Trees are also homes to other plants. Mosses and lichens grow on trunks and branches, and ferns may take root here, too. In the warm, moist tropics, many plants grow on trees. They include beautiful orchids, shiny cheese plants, climbing figs, and pretty flowering vines.

A sparrow hawk protects her young.

Enemies of Trees

Trees have many enemies. Lightning and fire can destroy them in a few minutes. Their leaves are food for many creatures, especially caterpillars, bugs, aphids and larger animals such as monkeys and sloths.

By midsummer, many leaves are full of holes. Often you cannot see what has been eating them. This is because caterpillars come out to feed at night, when there are no birds around to catch them. By day, they hide in crevices in the bark, or out of sight underneath the leaves.

You may find leaves with strange green or brown balls growing on them. These are galls. They are made by tiny gall wasps, which inject their eggs into the leaves. The leaf swells up around the wasp grubs to form a gall. If you break open the gall, you may find the tiny grub inside. Or you may

Oak marble galls made by the gall wasp.

The bark beetle larvae leave tunnels in the wood of the tree beneath the bark.

see the little hole through which the new wasp has escaped.

Beetles and their grubs can chew through wood. Beetle grubs chew long tunnels under the bark. The beetles may carry tree diseases from one tree to another.

Squirrels gnaw at bark, and deer rub their antlers on it, tearing off great strips. This allows dangerous fungi to get into the tree trunk and rot it.

An eyed hawk moth caterpillar feeding on a leaf. These caterpillars tend to come out at night to avoid predators.

The Death of a Tree

Fungus growing on a branch of a dead elder tree.

Trees may die if they are burned by fire or by lightning. If a large branch is torn off by the wind, diseases can get into the wood and may eventually kill a tree. This can also happen where the bark is damaged by squirrels, deer or beetles and their grubs.

Injuries allow fungi to get into a tree. The fungi send out millions of tiny white threads, which gradually dissolve the tree's **tissues**. The wood becomes soft and crumbly, and the tree rots. This is why many old trees are hollow.

Soft, rotting wood is useful to some animals, for it helps them to make nest holes or to probe for insect grubs.

A lesser-spotted woodpecker at its nest hole, with its beak stuffed full of insects.

Woodpeckers prefer to feed on the soft wood of rotting trees.

Many conifers and a few other trees have a special way of dealing with injuries. They produce a sticky gum, or resin, which seals the wound, preventing diseases and fungi from entering. So it is not surprising that some of the longest-living trees are conifers, such as the redwoods.

When a tree dies, the rotting log or stump provides food and shelter for many woodland animals. Fungi soon invade, and colorful toadstools appear. Centipedes, woodlice, earwigs, spiders and beetles and their grubs find shelter under the loose bark. They provide food for birds, skunks, badgers and shrews. Some animals, like raccoons, may spend the winter asleep in hollow logs. An old log soon becomes covered with mosses and ferns, providing new nooks and crannies for tiny creatures.

7
Learning More About Trees

Horse chestnut trees have compound leaves made up of several leaflets.

What Kind of Tree Is It?

If you want to find out what kind of tree you are looking at, you will need to look at its flowers, fruits and leaves. Does it have flowers or cones? Do the flowers grow singly, or in clusters? What color are they? How many petals, stamens and carpels do they have? What shape are the petals? What kind of fruits and seeds does it have? What shape are the leaves? Are they very simple, or are they made up of several smaller leaflets? Do the leaves grow in pairs on the twig, or one at a time? If you make a note of all these things, you will be able to look up your tree in a book and find out what it is.

Pressing Leaves and Flowers

Place some leaves or flowers between two pieces of absorbent paper like paper towels, add a layer of newspaper, and press the flowers between two boards. You can pull the boards tightly together by wrapping straps around them, or you can put them under a pile of heavy books.

When your plants are completely dry and flat, mount them carefully on a piece of cardboard, and label them. On the label you should write the name of the tree or flower, and where and when you found it.

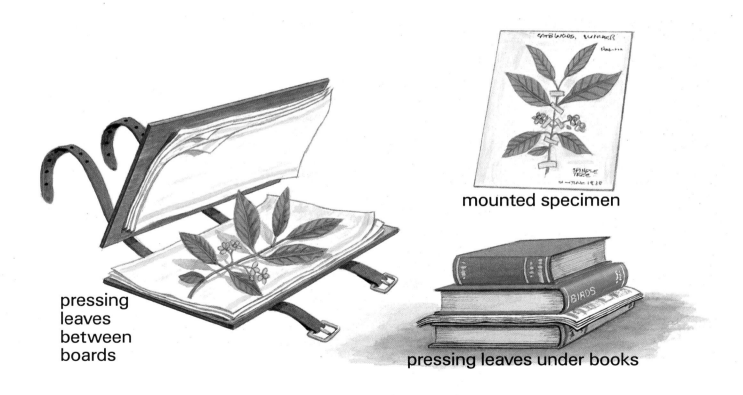

mounted specimen

pressing leaves between boards

pressing leaves under books

horse
chestnut

growing
seedlings

bark rubbing

Bark Rubbings

Different trees have different patterns on their bark. You can make an interesting picture with some strong paper and wax crayons. Hold the paper firmly over the bark and rub the crayon over the surface of the paper. This will create an effect like the texture of the bark.

Growing Tree Seedlings

Try growing trees from their fruits or seeds. You can place large seeds such as chestnuts or avocados in a vase over some water and keep it in a warm place.

Smaller seeds will grow in a pot containing special seed compost. Make a hole in the bottom of the pot and place it on a dish of gravel, so the water can drain through. Keep the compost moist by adding water to the dish, or by covering the pot with a plastic bag. Keep your seeds in a dark, warm place, such as a cupboard, until the young shoots begin to appear. Move the seedlings to a warm, sunny place, a window sill perhaps, and keep them well watered.

The Jeffrey pine tree has a pinkish brown colored bark with deep vertical cracks in it.

Glossary

Anther The upper part of a stamen containing the pollen.

Bark A hard, corky substance that forms the outer layer of a tree trunk or branch.

Bud scales Small, papery leaves that protect the delicate shoot or flower inside a bud.

Carbon dioxide A gas found in the air and used by plants to make their food by the process of photosynthesis.

Calyx The outer cover of a flower bud.

Carpel The part of the flower in which the seeds grow. The ovary, style and stigma are parts of the carpel.

Cells Tiny units of living matter.

Chlorophyll The green coloring in plants, which enables them to carry out photosynthesis.

Cones The reproductive parts of conifers, which produce pollen and eggs.

Conifers Plants that produce cones instead of flowers.

Crown The mass of branches above the main unbranched part of the tree trunk.

Deciduous Shedding the leaves in winter or during the dry season.

Evergreen Keeping the leaves all year round.

Fertilized To join pollen with the eggs of a plant to produce a seed.

Fruit The seed, together with the plant parts surrounding it, that is shed from its parent plant. For example, apples and oranges are fruits.

Fungus (plural fungi) Mushrooms, molds, toadstools and other plants that have no leaves, flowers or green color.

Hedgerow A thickly planted row of low trees and bushes forming the boundary of a field or road.

Nectar A sweet-smelling sugary liquid produced by plants to attract insects and other animals for pollination.

Needles Stiff, needle-shaped leaves.

Ovary The part of the flower that contains the plant's egg cells.

Oxygen A gas found in the air, and produced by plants during photosynthesis.

Photosynthesis The process by which plants make their own food from simple chemicals (carbon dioxide and water), using the energy of sunlight.

Pistil The female organ of a flower, formed of one or more carpels.

Pollination The transfer of pollen from the stamens to the stigma of a flower.

Resin Thick, sticky gum found in the trunks of some trees.

Sap The juice that runs through the stems of plants.

Seed leaves The first leaves produced by a new plant or **seedling**. Seed leaves are often used to store food in the seed.

Seeds The offspring of a plant.

Sepals The leaves that form the **calyx**.

Stamens The male parts of a flower. Stamens are made up of a stalk supporting a bag of pollen.

Stigma The sticky tip of a carpel, used to trap pollen.

Stomata Tiny holes in the surface of a leaf through which gases enter and leave.

Style The long, drawn-out tip of a carpel, which supports the stigma.

Tissues Groups of similar cells.

Trunk The thick, woody stem of a tree.

Finding Out More

Carolyn Boulton, *Trees*. Franklin Watts, 1984

Jennifer Coldrey, *Discovering Flowering Plants*, Bookwright Press, 1987

Herbert L. Edlin, *The Tree Key*. Scribner, 1985

Dougal Dixon, *A Closer Look at Jungles*, Gloucester Press, 1984

Bayard Hora (ed.), *The Oxford Encyclopedia of Trees of the World*. Oxford University Press, 1981

David Lambert, *Trees of the World*. Bookwright Press, 1986

Herbert Zim & Alexander Martin, *Trees* (Golden Guide series). Western Publ., 1952

Index

Animals 24, 25, 26, 34, 35, 36, 37, 38, 39

Bats 34
Birds 24, 25, 26, 34, 35, 39
Broad-leaved trees 10–11, 28, 32

China 9, 30
Chlorophyll 14
Coffee 30
Conifers 10, 12–13, 28, 32, 39

Forests 28–9
Fruit trees 22, 23, 24, 27, 31
Fungi 8, 37, 38, 39

India 30
Insects 22, 23, 34, 35, 36, 37, 38, 39

Kapok 25

Maple syrup 30
Mosses and lichens 35, 39

Nectar 23

Oils 30

Panama 29
Paper 32
Parts of a tree
    bark 8, 31, 42
    branches 8, 11, 19
    bud scales 11
    cones 8, 10, 12–13, 20–21, 22
    crown 19
    flowers 8, 10, 20–21, 22, 23, 40
    fruits 8, 24–25, 30
    leaves 8, 10, 13, 14–15, 16, 30, 31
    nuts 8, 30
    roots 8, 16–17, 19, 33
Photosynthesis 14–15, 17
Pollen 21, 22, 23
Pollination 21, 22–3, 24

Pressing leaves 40–1

Rain forests 29
Resin 33, 39

Seed leaves 18
Seedlings 18, 43
Spices,
    nutmeg 31
    cinnamon 31
Sri Lanka 30

Tea 30
Trees,
    apple 24, 30, 31
    bald cypress 28
    beech 11, 16
    bristlecone pine 8, 9, 39
    cherry 27, 30
    cocoa 29
    coconut palm 25
    cypress 13
    date palms 31
    elder 37
    elm 10
    fir 13

ghost gum 8, 9
ginkgo 9
hawthorn 24
hazel 25
holly 10, 24
horse chestnut 40
larch 13
laurel 10
magnolia 23
mangrove 29

maple 24, 25
oak 11, 18, 25, 26
olive 31
pine 13, 16, 28
poui 21
redwood 8, 12, 39
rubber 32
spruce 13
sycamore 25
tulip 23

willow 25
yew 13, 24
Tropical swamps 29
Tropical trees 28, 29, 30, 31, 32

United States 29

Windbreaks 27

Picture acknowledgments

All photographs are from Oxford Scientific Films by the following photographers: Caroline Aitzemuller 34; Jill Bailey frontispiece, 11 (right); G.I. Bernard 10, 18, 40; Neil Bromhall cover; Michael Brooke 33; Graham Cogbill 32; J.A.L. Cooke 14; E.R. Degginger 37 (left); Jack Dermid 16 (right), 43; David Fox 35; Michael Fogden 12, 30; John Gerlach 9; R.J.B. Goodale 8; Terry Heathcote 11 (left); Breck P. Kent 13 (left), 24 (right); Andrew Lister 19; C.C. Lockwood 28 (right); G.A. Maclean 15, 22; T.C. Middleton 28 (left); Sean Morris 29; Richard Packwood 24 (left); D.J. Saunders 39; Tim Shepherd 13 (right), 16 (left) 26, 36; D.J. Stradling 21; Anna Walsh 27, 38; P. and W. Ward 31; Barrie E. Watts 37 (right).